ColoringBook

By Banana leaves

....

Colorist's Name

....

Date

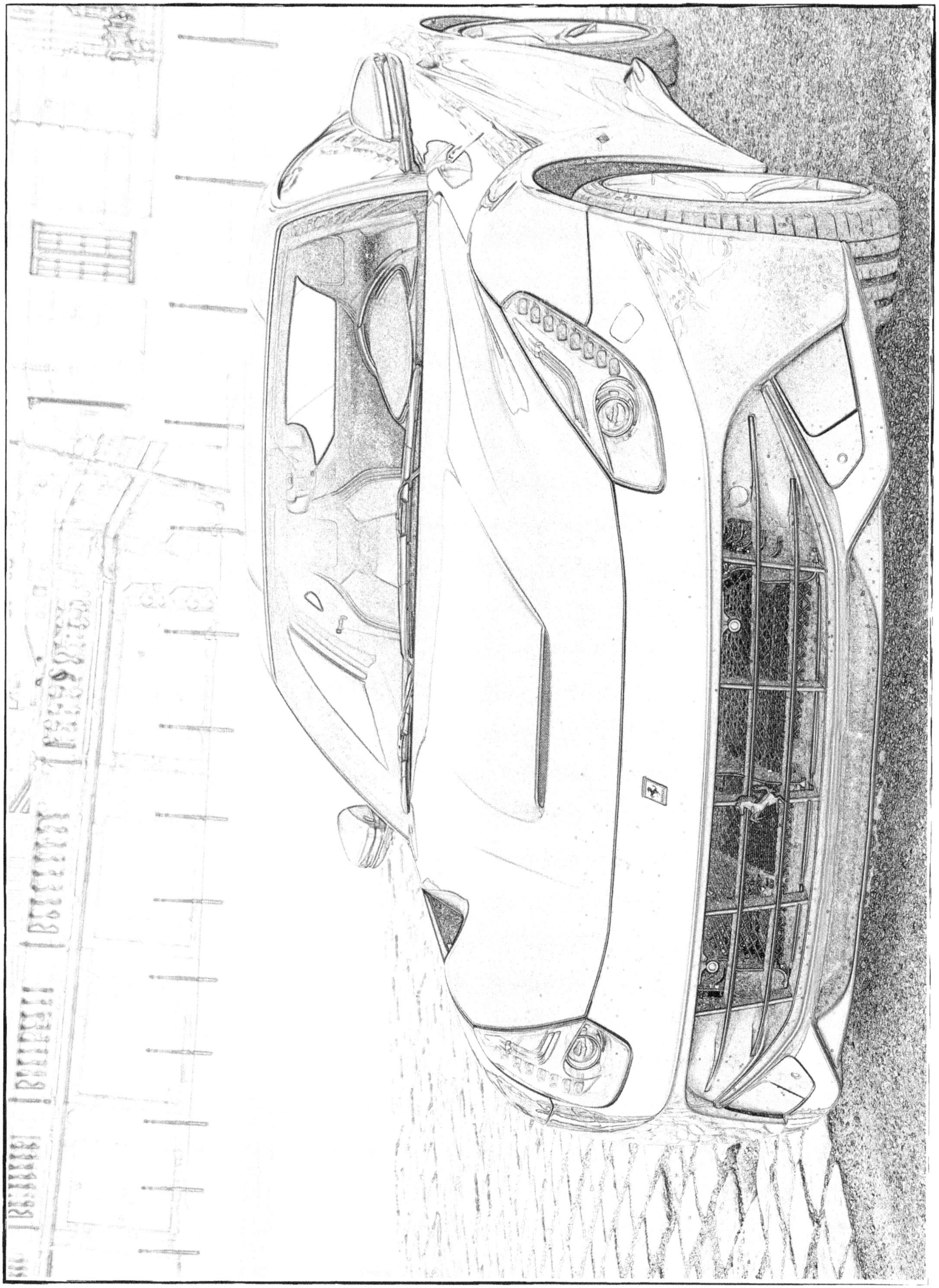

LIGHTNING

E14 CED

FI IRAK

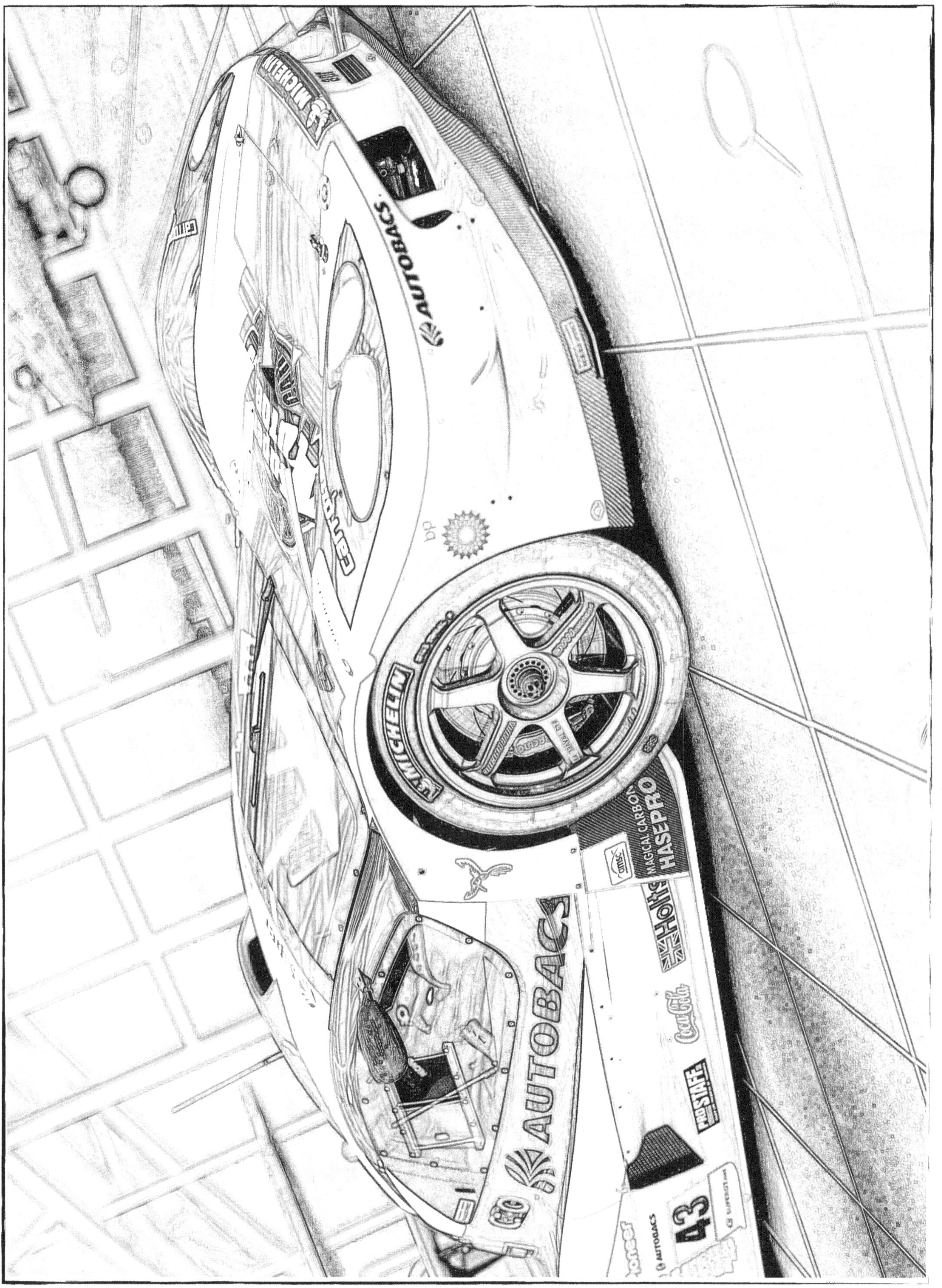
AUTOBACS
MICHELIN
MAGICAL CARBON
HASEPRO
bp
43

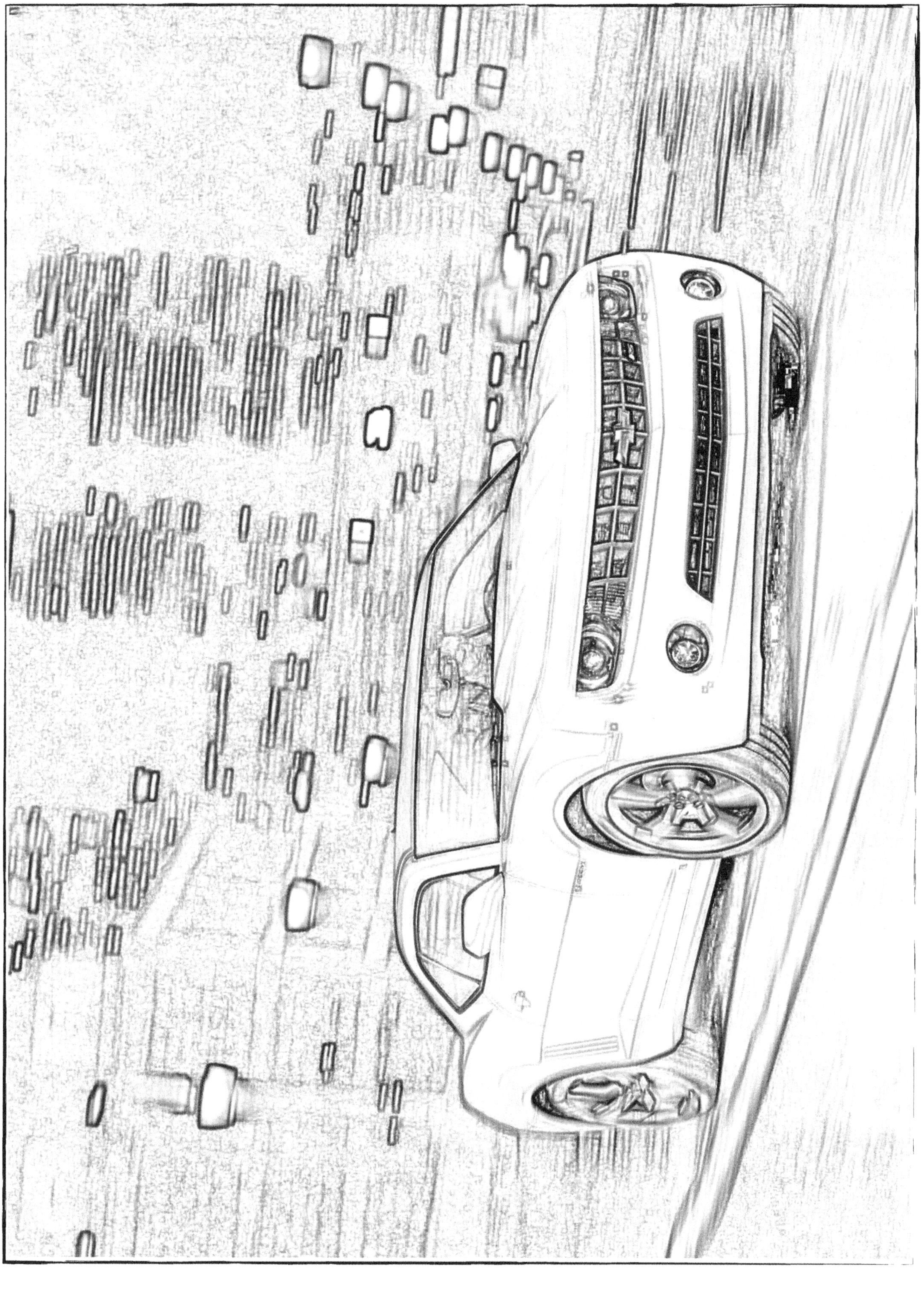

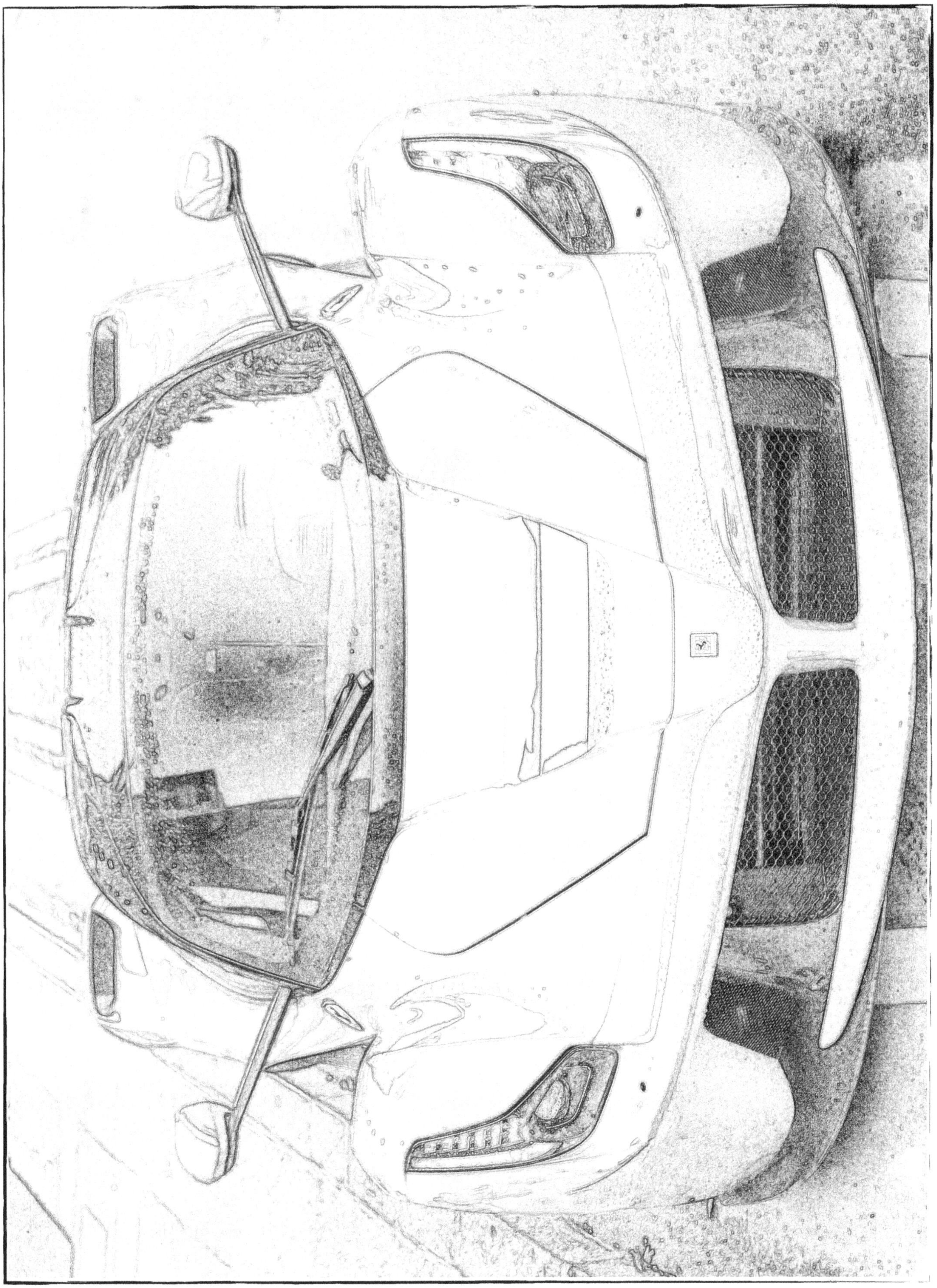

LADURÉE
LADURÉE

SN13 FNJ

16
18
824
CHRISTIES
BATTERY
DATE.COM
PEN

betsafe

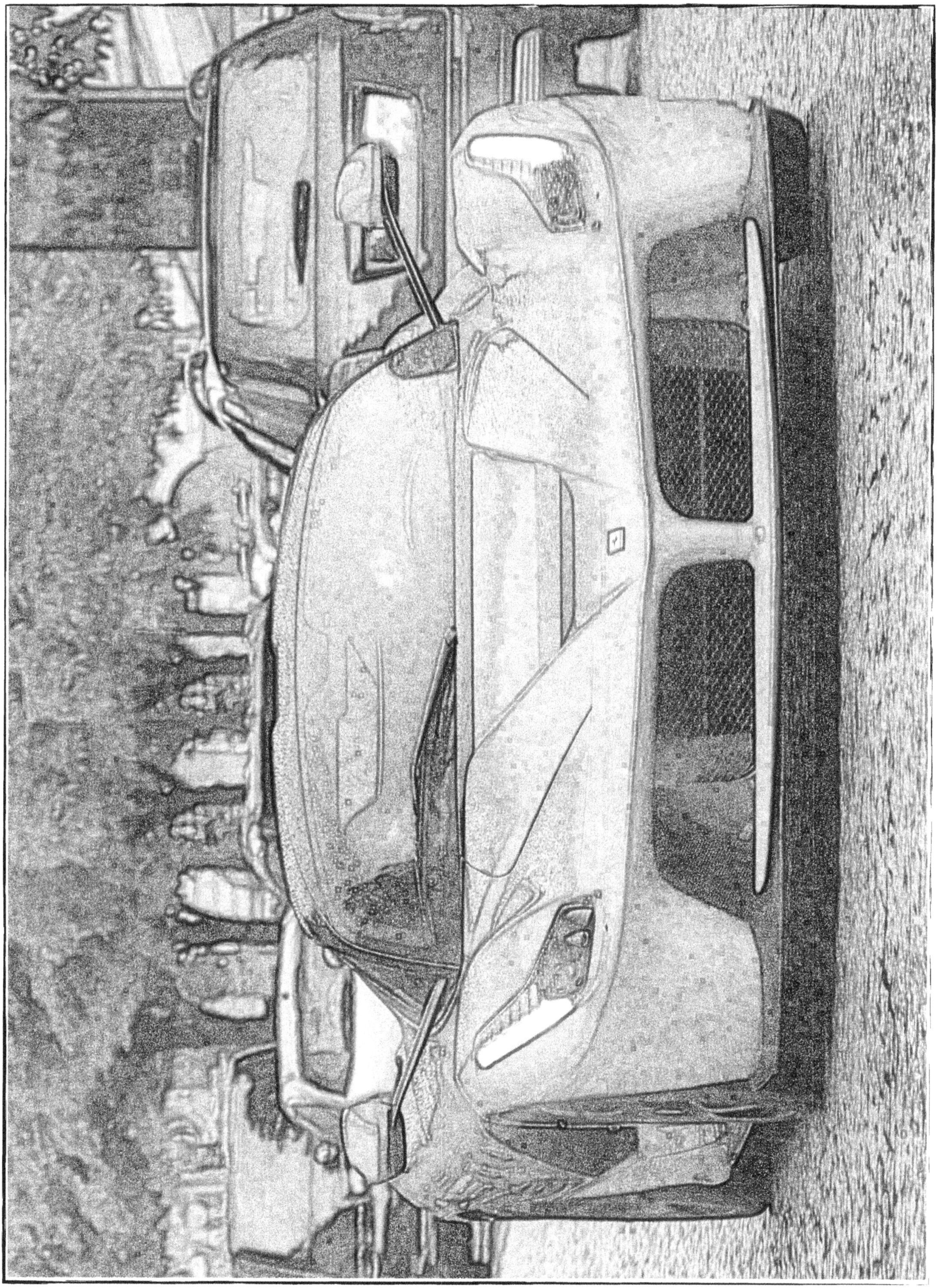

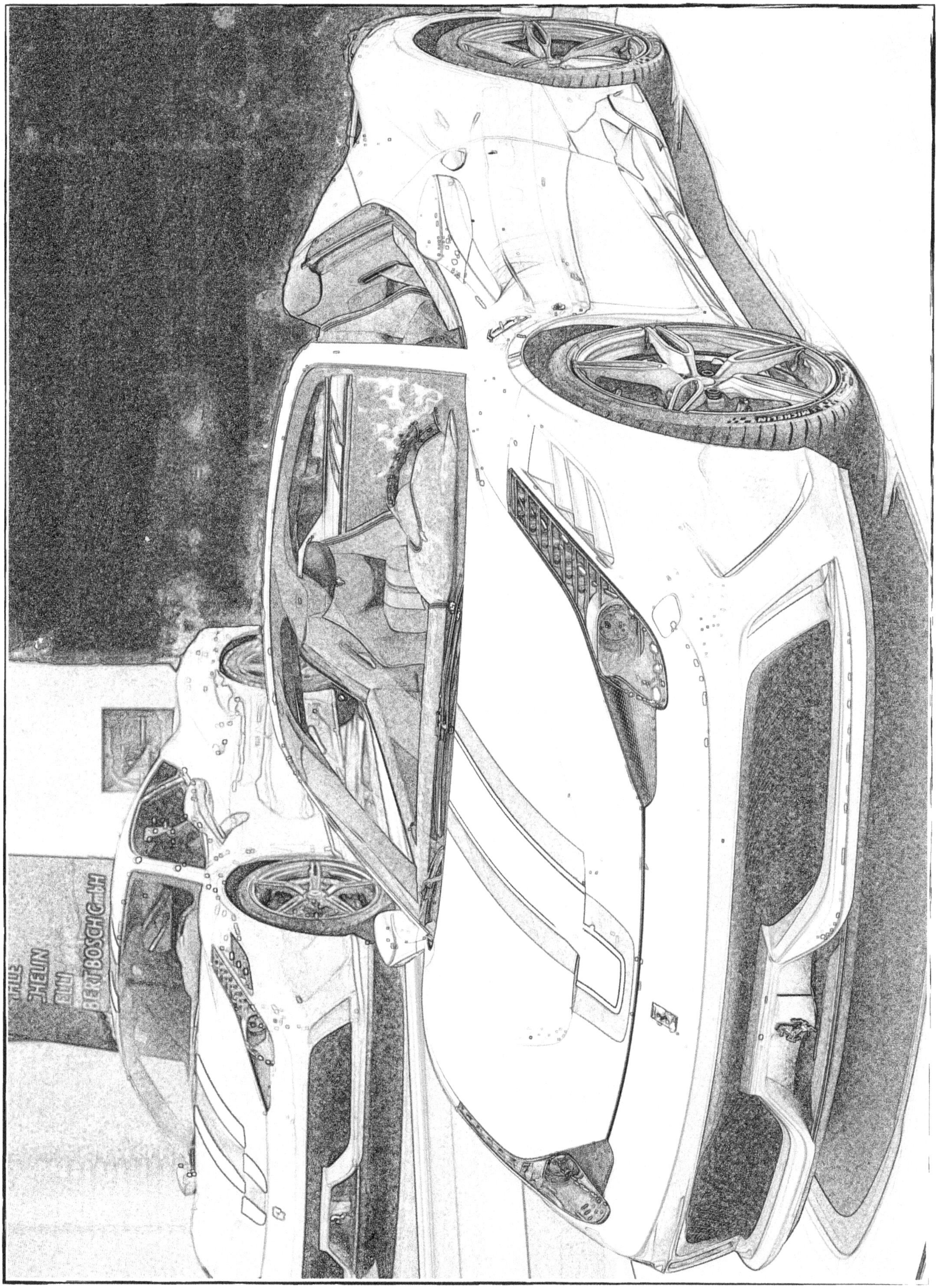

FOUR SEASONS HOTEL
George V

LJ62 DGX

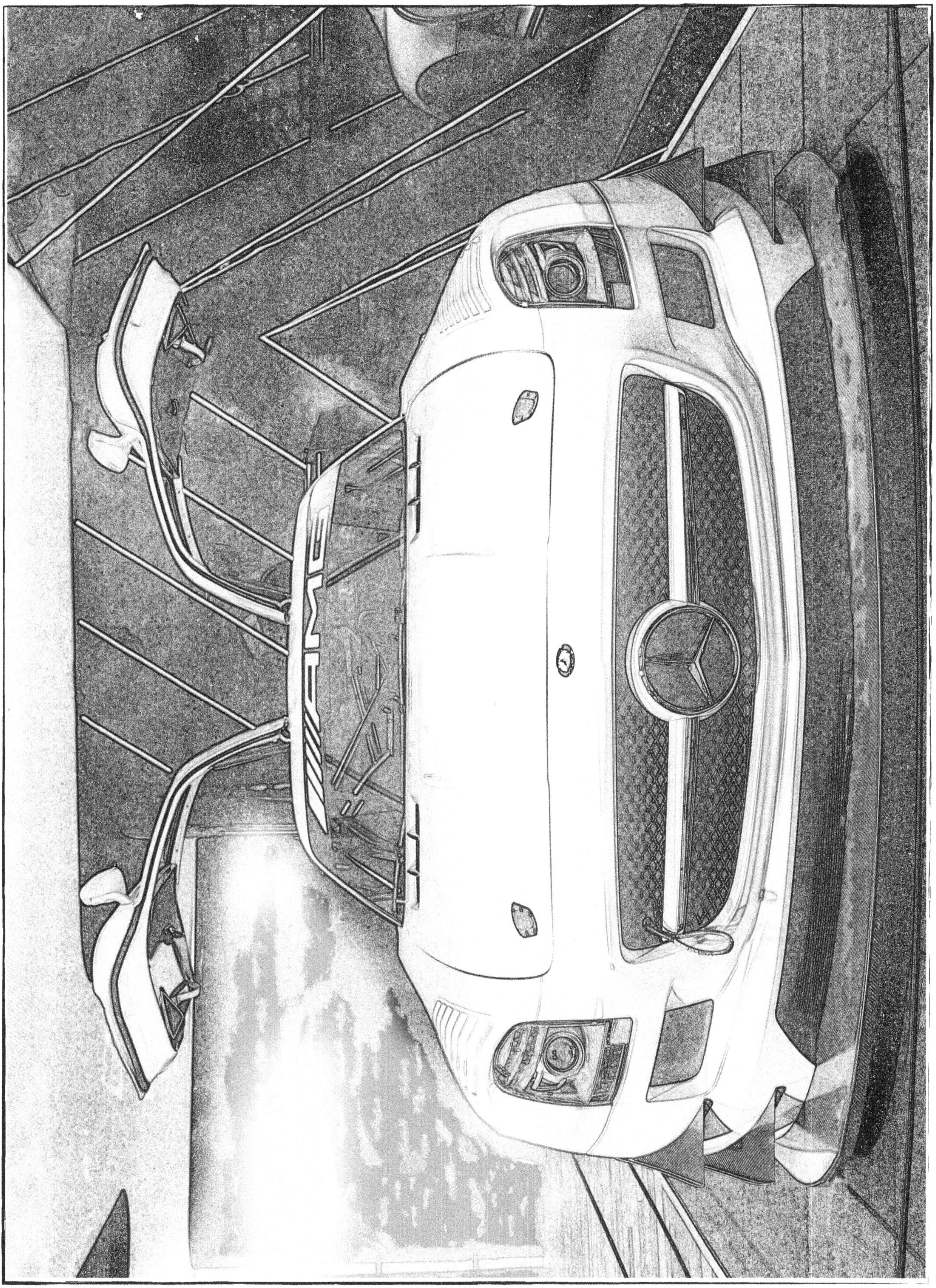
AMG

153
FASTER
TORK
Sabelt

Made in the USA
Coppell, TX
25 July 2020

31670623R00037